AF207879

Catalogue of Burnt Text

Timothy David Orme

BlazeVOX [books]

Buffalo, New York

Catalogue of Burnt Text by Timothy David Orme
Copyright © 2009

Published by BlazeVOX [books]

Printed in the United States of America

Book design by Geoffrey Gatza

First Edition
ISBN: 9781935402558
Library of Congress Control Number 2009925635

BlazeVOX [books]
14 Tremaine Ave
Kenmore, NY 14217

Editor@blazevox.org

publisher of weird little books

BlazeVOX [books]

blazevox.org

2   4   6   8   0   9   7   5   3   1

B   X

Acknowledgments

Thank you to the following print and online journals in which some of these poems first appeared, often in various forms: *Interim, GutCult, Word For / Word, Muse Apprentice Guild.*

Also many thanks to those who have helped along the way, whether directly or indirectly: Janet Holmes, Martin Corless-Smith, Mia Wright, Helen Lojek, Jodi Chilson.

For My Sister

Catalogue of Burnt Text

whereupon alone by the leaving
tree I sit, dewdrops / flowers afoot, and watch the sky's endless climbing between leaves

I write

       Ipsentius

to you

One says there is no time for *x*, and immediately begins explaining time as existing on an immeasurable plane consisting of motion and the human self revolving around a particular location in the universe that will continue to exist only as long as both motion and the self exist—all of which one says is (of course) inexplicable with words and does not stop the arms from reaching.

To Ipsentius

How can I climb you down the clouds

Rounding mine eye   wide
I call for your sight & strength

Sky
No other eyes through only mine do you have seams

Down into & call up the one who colors the seas
Sky   how wide the world is

> spring
> & he wakes
> up walking
> outside bare
> feet in dew
> pulling from
> the trees fresh
> leaves

I write you not enough—for now you exist only when I write your name.

Time has taken me: by the speed of the sky and the earth I have lost my self.

If self exists as owner of a body and space, can one lose it?

If the self exists on an unknowable plane as part of the mind, it must be possible to lose the self

      as one loses time.

All I can find is the time to produce this letter—-a postulation, a pursuit—

      all I do.

O Roman poet, I write you because you are all that appeases my mind.

But, my words are only words (ego tibi aliquid de meis scriptis mittam. nihil erat absoluti.) Which may come as no surprise.

<u>a</u> <u>spring</u> <u>scene</u> <u>of</u> <u>waters</u> <u>arriving</u>

The Motion

I

if I could move wont to another
    & if walking could in lay
at any moment in any thing
  & fix mine self an object yet
this motion
~~in~~ am me
~~was~~ all my whole

~~II~~

I have watched a hand write words at its will. Its curve and movement determines: creation or destruction in one firm line. Self made an object as words on the page.

A removable object.

When will you be arriving here? Give me notice, for I will enjoy preparing for your arrival.

My beloved companion, the sun is assimilating in the distance as the clouds pass. I want them to stay for me.

For you I wish the rain. I wish you the flecks of dirt that rise towards the clouds for a moment, only to fall back from whence they came.

Man falls back into dirt but not you,

out past the lengths of the clouds and borders of the skies.

midday
rain clouds
carpet above
the blooming
moonflower

seeds in his hands
with folded fingers

gritty gait

One finds the opening of clouds like the opening of books, so that in the beginning words and meanings fly about as a rain that bathes and gently nourishes the bending leaves, and one then realizes the opening of clouds is nothing like the opening of books, but rather like the closing of the watery eyes that continue to run and run

the   woman soaking in
water   up to her shoulders hair
trickles   curly & down
down   her back water   with
the   breaths she takes   on her
fence   a bird shaking its feathers

When in water or shade: ᾽Λκεα.

Feelings in motion release them selves.

Arm of tree.

Flower stem.

Vegetal division.

Ipsentius— There has been a rain, such that I have tried to catch it my hands and have been unable to do so.

o leander span your petals
more extend & up your stalk
come freshet waves running
water overwhelms your roots

ego etiam nunc codem in loco
iaco sine sermone ullo, sine cogitatione ulla

(yet)

voice

finds its way

interdum lacrimae pondera vocis habent

(these)

———————

& when these sometimes fire burns down clouds
dissolves itself into a streak fallen from thee
aether thus spake an untranslatable language
an one to hear its tone fulfills

Spring Notes on Ipsentius

non queo plura scribere nec est quod scribam

I say the word azimuth,
pronouncing all three

syllables, noticing how
none of them
                    seems to leave
my mouth.

Give me first the leavéd tree and the seedlings blown to foreign places for rest.

A tree reaching. Balancing one way with the other.

I am too tired to reach any longer.

When the cold comes ~~it~~ I must sleep and wait to wake and stretch again.

licet tibi, ut scribis, significarim ut ad me venires, <id> dono tamen et intellego te istic
prodesse, hic ne verbo quidem levare me posse.

(that which is lit will flicker)

Wind from a mouth – words

But can they blow themselves away without this being called self destruction and instead being called self amelioration—

wind springing up to create its own passage home—

or

(you make me gullible)

vidi ego pampineis oneratam vitibus ulmum,
   quae fuerat saevi fulmine tacta Iovis.

    & then the winter forest   one
    cold & white except one   tree
    growing greenleaves

I think nothing of it for the fire flushed to ashes. I must seek warmth.

    not knowing
    how it will be
    blown out
    the candle wick
    enjoys burning

I cannot stay in the same location for any length of time, for the although the mind
becomes content with a single set of thoughts, the eye desires light on a new location.

sees   one word writ on waves
or hears   three chanted in moonlight

quantumcumque tamen praeconia nostra valebunt
carminibus vives tempus in omne meis.

SUMMER SONGS

That so our sweetly temper'd song
Nor be too ~~short, nor~~ seeme to long.

rays dissipate into
west & blue

round an island
up come birds

an(d) instant
           song

Nothing more than

the silence of the hyacinth isles

free and full of song

I have placed the full leaved

trees behind for I will

always find or see

will always see the leaves

by light or shade

content

on the top of
the rock mountain

one will
            not fall

finding
a stream

I find
I do

what
a stream will

as it is carved by water

the rock between
the river shores

carves the waters clear

stop
& rest
& sit

beneath

the leaves
of the tamarind tree

seedpods play

their tune
I am losing

strength

to sing
to long

where was this
land alone

where I was
walking

&

where was I
where I sing

if only this
be what I wish

ENCHIRIDION

I. PREFACE PRESENTED

in woo(/r)ds en light
diaphanous lay – green fog shroud

The influence of the him to be
wise of himself by
the way the same

II. CONTROVERSIES IN PLACE OF THUS AN HANDBOOK

When I attempts
pricks hands the black that
mine all names mine I

A pinecone

III. NONE OTHER THAN WHAT WE VIEW WE WORRY

What/When other can we

Dried green to red
its fallen black barrels
on brown ground ashed white

I lost in them then
Neither front nor back seeing
But still se & seeing
the all of what encompasses

So sat I round
What colors were willed

IV. ONE ASPECT OF THIS

~~Strewn accross the fields will they grow~~
~~They hide too fat behind fallen trees levitating~~
~~We there more would I~~
~~Knew more of I would~~
~~I believe I found myself in this~~
I believe we all find our selves in this

V. OTHER ASPECTS OF THIS

sheets blown in wind

  torn

argu

       fad

crease

<u>catalogue</u> <u>of</u> <u>burnt</u> <u>text</u> (<u>inquisitions</u>)

why such a name

why names

whence the Latin poem

where the translation

why this feigned talk of movement when one is certainly standing still

why the tree

what songs voice

where is such space

why sound without rhyme

why sound without rhythm

whos counting meter

why the dappling on my window

how much longer will I wait

why the lean towards what

whos watching

why this construction

why all this why all this again

thoughts and remembrances

brid

stop this   start again

bird fly you in a tree   singme sweet

one wishes to build a bridge

                                              over
every thing   is over

no

                                              everything
is beginning

                                              none other than you can I hear

for I am

                                              blind

then close your eyes & sing

Welkin faire
& welkin High
sith I reache
I touch thee
eye

don't believe that

                                      or this
                    you   don't believe

anything   any thing

voice from throat

                                      it begetteth fathoms

ask it   (or sing it)

Why does the   nightengale sing
nightingale sing   to expand
it is   a voice
a beautiful sight   the voice of night
running words along   space relateth into song
so thick you can   see them come
see them shake   see them flutter
the leaves   their wings

these   gentle auspices   those

                                        (or) the sky

only in my dream can I reach it

                                        (this isn't about dreams)

then what is it about

the day   the day
the song   the sky

but the sky

                crepuscular   (tell yourself you're over it and you are)

the woodlands

                                        they are as far as low

                                        (or) to run again at a fast pace

do you pace yourself?

                                        I walk back
                                        and forth

then that would indicate different speeds?

                                        I only think in different directions

I need some time to think   I need some space

                like I said

redeunt in carmina vires then write it

I was then
what I will
be still now

               yes   I will read it

Where's my hellebore?

wan   (or)   wane

heu   heu

bonny sweet   silence of this summer day

what is the body   (but)   an extension of the mind
imagine the body   (and)   watch it vanish

what are you reading?   words
                                             words
                                             words

damn you birds   be quiet   you damn birds

                           come again

                           heare me

adew   flowers at my feet

Catalogue of woods   of fields
            of forests   of feelings

                                   1. log
                                   2. sod
(trod)   3. maelstrom   (folderol)

what needs I another   when I have you
when I have my self   what needs I another

another re   turn to the ancients
                                    (for solidity – or the
                                    impression thereof)

(or) for to translate   Martial

You weep once   you have done that which
you love most   you want the action
so why are you in sorrow   for the deed do you
regret it or   weep
instead   because

            the action is over

or an earlier bedrock

                          fragments of some monolithic Greek stone

When Zeno finished speaking with the group the young Socrates spoke first, pointing out the apparent contradictions

Therefore you understand the book, Socrates—

        yes, you are trying to mislead us, Zeno

                —and at the same time you have not
                grasped the truth of the book.

(cadence)   (credence)

        When a dream
        becomes

        too frightening
        I tell myself

        enough
        & although

        still frightened

        wake

extended catalogue of burnt text

Tomorrow

Epistle to J.

Homeric Hymn

Market List – garlic, mushrooms, mandarin

Letter to Lawyer(s) ? – implicate passive voice that implies 'you'

crux

slide sideways on sofa

read – alternating herbert with heidegger (25:1)

Omitted text

summersault incident

sex

signified(s)

stingy thistle (no need for explication)

> [what was not a turning point
> was merely a point – a spire
> I hung my shoe on]

Returns

non sum ego qui fueram

Yet neither was Descartes.
Nietzsche may have falsely accused.

There is the saying it and there is my believing it

Neither of which I know to be fully true

(stand atop a stone & sigh)

like colors from afar
mere rhythm smeared
but breathing upfront as buttoned
a pear opens peculiar robes

I need food &   my hand shakes.

The wind blows &   the paper shakes.

The journey does not stop because the movement [of the individual] stops.

I cannot separate movement from light. Mine inspiration. Round me.

What more or better to do but watch the light moving: differently over the same stone?

snakes shed skin I shell |shall|

home not home
but a covering |cowering|
covering a home

limbs a part
I extend out
seams soft skin |seems|

could crack along
brown could grow |would|
green end could

seek suture

Come w Me

strive I to be
of thee soul
a wanderer

———————

cherubs will come w me
the cherubs will swim in
air around (&) me
of an floating current

wind will come w me
will wash the rain in
one direction west of
for these are forests falld

earth will come w me
the earth will rift its back
a stand I that an higher than
sand that held surface water

blood will come w me
will filter run & seep
its direction south
sowed a circle in its sky

cur scribam, doci. vobiscum cupio quolibet esse modo.

Epistle for M.

You who have me thinking about the break
who have me contented that defines
but where is some such wider
in burnt dictionary capitol or dome

Legend of Unknown Origin

when he left

same day

in sky
routine
home

water
down to
the river
to retrieve

his return
both for why
for what

she waited

she would
sometimes
climb
the mountains
to watch

him coming

until one

day
of waiting

when she turned

she turned

to stone

and the earth and the land changeth often his colour.

A natural force is involved for one color to collide with another.

Spring orange green bobbing from the branches.

An unimaginable ~~movement~~ moment as the two cleave:

> the fallen & lying
> oranges in field
> green

The taking of two for one to exist

Or desire. |osiris dies|

Osiris Dies

up osiers now sing
with him & heare calcined
the more your yellow leaves

stir strong & struggle
his capsule wood conseale him with
will what resound through

consort then in one song
one him to flowing out
sweet & swaying then washed

   I got me this tree & cut it gone
   drag it back to home its

   asked can sap suture its
   scent becomes a palace can

   aspens sit
   so still is there but one

With the leaves scatter   so do thoughts I write them   as they   now brief   and fast scribbles

Praetulerim scriptor delirus   inersque videri, dum mea   delectent mala   me vel denique fallant,   quam sapere et ringi.

Can you remember

   what a leaf is if

its veins

   your own hand

so many to touch

   the air the wind the sky

so many when they wave

     they wave
& they trickle

   they weave

theyre hands in & out

    sewing the sky

together they turn them selves

     away a hand

withdraws from the trees

   reach

Marygold

on solid ground soft
wet and unfrost

you fragrant orange buttercup
you day rayflowr

a slit suns aperture
from grownds reeds

&

your sacred radiance
your nurley scent

no faden bloom but on floreshen

Epistle for M.

Mocking light towards
I know not what again

caps black bed frame

I was not yours you said
nor in language nor house

such an old sink
such a new toothbrush

A Soul's Finding: Segment of a Lost Myth, Suspected an Ending Scene

————

Suddenly
   dawn

swiftly   but
          a

ll o   er
  nd lost alone
d n   bl
swallowing waters
::   ::
             sea

               rocking.

        ————

n ne yet know what w s brought
on   sea's horizon   day t
         s me still look
at sunset see n nly   then
  waves cradling light
within its   waves possibly
boat a d   a figure
not kno g t   igure flowing
    alive r   dead   lowing

56

[   ]

What does the tree offer? It leaves

[us]   changes

       [us] as we grow accustomed.

          me vix misereque sustento.

If I stand here long enough even these mountains shall fall.

Motion does not stop because you cannot see it.

[(Surely) I am somewhere exaggerating.]

Walking through the woods I heard the cry of the song sparrow which I associated with the written word and its loathsomeness, its long notes drawn out, its cry for attention.

Nemo aliquid recognoscat, nos mentimur omnia.

Do not struggle, when I leave

and cannot be found, even in mine letters' words. Do not reread them for you may

remember them.

You do not need to understand or remember. Already

you know what I say.

Translations

ego tibi aliquid de meis scriptis mittam. nihil erat absoluti. / I shall be sending you a sample of my writings. I have nothing quite finished.

Λκεα / silence, healing.

ego etiam nunc codem in loco iaco sine sermone ullo, sine cogitatione ulla / I am stuck here with no one to talk to and nothing to talk about.

interdum lacrimae pondera vovis habent / tears sometimes have the strength of spoken words.

non queo plura scribere nec est quod scribam / I can't write any more, nor have I anything to write about.

licet tibi, ut scribis, significarim ut ad me venires, <id> dono tame et intellego te istic podesse, hic ne verbo quidem levare me posse. / I may have suggested to you, as you say, that you should join me; but I gave that up, and realize that you are helping me where you are, whereas you could do nothing even verbally to lighten my load.

vidi ego pampineis oneratam vitibus ulum, / quae fuerat saevi fulmine tacta Iovis. / I have seen an elm laden with the tendrils of a vine even after it had been blasted by the thunderbold of angry Jove.

quantumcumque tamen praeconia nostra valebunt / carminibus vives tempus in omne meis. / Yet so far as my praise has power, thou shalt live for all time in my song.

reduent in carmina vires / strength returns to my song

non sum ego qui fueram / I am not what I was

cur scribam, doci. vobiscum cupio quolibet esse modo. / Why I write I have told you. I am eager to be with you in some fashion. no matter how.

Praetulerim scriptor delirus inersque videri, dum mea delectent mala me vel denique fallant, quam sapare et ringi. / I should prefer to be thought a foolish and clumsy scribbler, if only my failings please, or at least escape me, rather than be wise and happy.

me vix misereque sustento. / I keep going with difficulty and wretchedness.

Nemo aliquid recognoscat, nos mentimur omnia. / No one should take this seriously, for it is all a lie.

Made in the USA
Monee, IL
07 July 2026